GHOST TOWN POETRY
ANTHOLOGY
Volume Two
2004 – 2014

Celebrating Ten Years
Of The
Ghost Town Poetry Open Mic
In Collaboration With
Cover To Cover Books
Vancouver, Washington

Edited By
Christopher Luna and Toni Partington

GHOST TOWN POETRY ANTHOLOGY
Volume Two
2004 – 2014

Celebrating Ten Years of the Ghost Town Poetry Open Mic in collaboration with Cover To Cover Books, Vancouver, Washington

Editors
Christopher Luna and Toni Partington

Book Design
Toni Partington

Cover Art
Christopher Luna and Toni Partington

Photo of the Editors
Julian Nelson

Published By
Printed Matter Vancouver
Vancouver, Washington
www.printedmattervancouver.com
printedmattervancouver@gmail.com

ISBN-13: 978-0615938899 (Printed Matter Vancouver)
ISBN-10: 0615938892

GHOST TOWN POETRY Volume Two has arrived!
Here's what writers had to say about
Ghost Town Poetry Volume One:

Ghost Town Poetry is such a genuinely remarkable carousel of what poetry can do that if it were sent out on another Voyager mission and discovered by extraterrestrials it would allow them to know what being a human being on the earth was like. There are so many good, well-crafted poems in this anthology that each one calls out for attention because, as William Stafford said, "poetry is about a certain kind of attention," which *Ghost Town* delivers.

You are taken somewhere which bypasses the brain's stifling seat of reason, and yet are given unforgettable lines, like Kyle David Congdon's "I know forever about the unfinished endless visions," followed shortly by "you need to breathe, Butterfly," which sums up the totality, setting out travail and treatment better than a PhD thesis or the Diagnostic and Statistical Manual of Mental Illness. There is the vastness of the intelligence in Alex Birkett's "Avoiding the Light," which rescues humanity from its isolating, isolated morass of smothering morality by celebrating our pleasure principle, not "east of Eden" but somewhere left of "whoopi." And then to turn around in "Styx" and in a few short lines juggle the see saw transition from tenderness to the heart's rage, left me wanting more. Even porn can't do that.

I just wanted to stay in the Ghost Town poems and go back and forth like a child in a swing.

Dennis McBride
Author of *Looking for Peoria* and *Killing the Mockingbird*
& Ghost Town Poetry Open Mic regular
2011

Everything's up to date in Vancouver (Washington) and this anthology of poetry is made up of poetry read in the town's hippest reading series from 2004 through 2010. I'm happy to say the series is still going, attracting poets from every part of the Northwest and beyond. The reading series curators, Christopher Luna and Toni

Partington, have made a bargain with the public, and one of their tenets is to let nothing second rate appear in their book. Thus we get the best work from each poet, even the ones famous on a national level, like Michael Rothenberg or David Meltzer (Meltzer, after all, was one of the original New American Poets anointed by Donald M. Allen in an influential 1960 anthology, so he knows firsthand how a good anthology can change a person's life). I was awed to think that a single book could give me an in-the-round picture of a single American city, like the old modernist classics such as Spoon River Anthology, but here it goes again.

Rob Gourley's "US 250" describes, in broken, dynamic rhythms, a favorite "cruise," in which, through the magic of memory, once again "we jump across the creek/ to reach the pumphouse and roam the slanting cowpaths." Another Vancouverite, Bernadette Barrio, opens up the world of children inching closer to adulthood and the pains of the mother as she prides themselves on their growth, while at risk of losing "that child-like charm they possess." Reading lines like this make me wonder if sometimes I overthink things and in doing so, miss out on some of the more poignant experiences of life. "I am a rich man, and I am surrounded by beauty," writes co-editor Luna in a stirring preface.

The mind of the poet is frequently topsy-turvy. Perhaps that is why we turn to poetry in times of economic and cultural challenge such as today. Luna and Partington have done a sterling job gathering together the best work of many poets I've never heard of and sending their wisdom all across the world like a "coastal spirit courier, a rain-free olive branch."

Kevin Killian
Author of *Argento Series*, *Impossible Princess*, and *Spreadeagle*
Editor of *My Vocabulary Did This to Me: The Collected Poetry of Jack Spicer*
August 2012

Order Vol 1,*Ghost Town Poetry: Cover To Cover Books 2004-2010 Poems from the Ghost Town Open Mic* from your local independent bookstore or from Cover to Cover Books in Vancouver, WA, contact mail@covertocoverbooks.net or call 360-993-7777.

📖

DRYAS MARTIN – February 23, 1936 – July 12, 2011

Dryas Martin, wife of Jim Martin and bright light to all who knew her, brought the Ghost Town community lively stories and much laughter. We were entertained and delighted with her tale of Tiggy the cat, who found adventure in the oddest of places. Tiggy was as thoughtful and philosophical as Dryas, and at times we had to wonder if these adventures were a clever snapshot of Dryas' life. Combined with her riddles, infectious smile, and lilting voice, we were the privileged ones. We miss her deeply.

**Jewels of the Night
By Dryas Martin**

As Tiggy loved to count the clouds in the early afternoons, at night he watched the stars. And he wondered if the sun now shone upon the moon.

... Or was the moon *itself* alight! A great lantern hung up high, to light the lands below as it shone down from the sky!

Hours passed him by, as he thought about it all.

... But who could put it there? How could it be hung ...? And, if not hung, what held it up ... ? Why did it not fall ... ? Unless it wasn't that at all!

Perhaps the moon was just a huge yellow balloon, blown far up by turret winds ... and far away ....

Yet, again, thought Tig — if so far away, why was it so big!

He thought about the moon as he thought about the sun, and about most things, pondering on each thought till another one would come.

There was no end to thinking! And at heart he knew — there was no better thing to do — whether one was right or wrong, or just a little right, or a wee bit wrong. — What mattered was to do it.

📖

JACK McCARTHY – May 23, 1939 – January 17, 2013

Generous genius, spoken word icon, amazing talent, proud husband and father, and beautiful soul are a few of the ways we can describe Jack. A prolific, supportive mentor who loved to reach out and touch poetry firmly and gently with word caresses, Jack dedicated his life to the word. His work inspired so many, and has left us with an empty space that we are unable to fill. Meeting Jack was like catching up with an old friend and picking up the conversation where it left off, never missing a beat. He was forever generous with feedback, always honest, and willing to bring new poets into the light. Oh Jack, your words and spirit live on in so many of us.

A sincere thank you to Carol McCarthy, who has so lovingly kept Jack's poems and memory alive in the hearts of poets near and far. Carol's dedication to Jack's legacy proves that love has endured the loss of a piece of her heart, and will continue on in the spirit of what they shared.

"This one is a favorite of mine ... it brought tears when he wrote it in 1993, and boy does it bring them now! It's also worth noting that since he passed, I've seen hawks in the oddest of places – a "Fenway hawk" a week after he passed, at the Charlestown Navy Yard after the marathon bombings, by the pool on Cape Cod when I was thinking how wonderful life with my sons and husband is, on Thompson Island in the Boston Harbor Islands on one of my first days working there ... it goes on and on. I almost know he'll be there when I look up. Thank you so much for honoring him with your dedication."

Kathleen Chardavoyne, Jack's daughter

Introduction to the poem by Jack McCarthy:
It was one of those crystalline January days
that can be so cold, the kind of day when you see hawks
sitting in trees along the Mass Pike, facing into the sun.

I was driving my daughter Kathleen back to college,
and from time to time I'd point out the kind of tree
a hawk would like to sit in.

After three or four trees she asked,
"What is this thing with hawks?

Do you think you were a hawk
in a previous life or something?"

I smiled and said, "Perhaps,"
and talked no more of hawks.
But on the long ride home alone
I decided she was almost right, that

I'll come back as a hawk
By Jack McCarthy

and maybe some day, as I drift upon an updraft
the top of your blonde head will catch my eye
maybe as you jog along a country road
and my hawk heart will pump a simple
unfamiliar signal

not kill-and-eat, although there's something
in it like my feeling for the prey, that it
was good to kill and good to eat
but that it's over now

not sleep because the sun's still high
but there is something in it
that is like sleep

not mate because it's not that time, there is
no other hawk in sight; not feed-your-young
because I have no young to feed
yet there is something in it
about mating, about young

not fly-great-distances across the path of sun
because I'm where I'm at 'til I get cold
still, there is something of
great distances about it

not play-at-aerobatics with a raven
although there is something in it about with

Requiring no action, it will be gone as quickly as it came
and being hawk, I'll never think of it again

A shadow passing on the edge of consciousness
might nudge you to glance up,
and, squinting in the sun
you'll see me, dark and sharp
motionless but exquisitely mobile
sliding sideways down the bright blue sky,
your young blue eyes discerning separation
of the feathers
in my wingtips.
Any remembering
will be done by you.

Contents

Foreword

It's been a busy three years since the first edition of *Ghost Town Poetry* hit the streets in 2011. In all the flurry of book and coffee sales, signings, workshops, readings, art classes, author group events and mixers, one event has remained constant and steadfast for years: the second Thursday at seven PM.

Each month we here at Cover to Cover Books bring out the folding chairs and the podium, the microphone stand and the amplifier. Some months we used to say to each other, "The weather's awful" or "We're close to a holiday, do you think we need to set out all the chairs?"

And each month, we do need to set out all the chairs, even the heavy, awkward, uncomfortable and ugly orange plastic ones.

We have seating for about forty people in our little store, and every second Thursday, every chair is filled, and more. It's always standing-room-only at the Ghost Town Poetry open microphone. None of our other events, however well-attended, boast that kind of crowd. It's not the bookstore venue that draws them in, it's the series hosts, Christopher Luna and Toni Partington.

Over the past three years, our poets have come and gone, moved into the area or away, brought new life into the world and buried loved ones, published chapbooks and broadsheets and books. The community that is Ghost Town Poetry celebrates and mourns together, but above all they care about and for each other.

We may provide the home, but Chris and Toni have made the family that lives within its sheltering, powerful walls of words.

Congratulations on this new edition of Ghost Town Poetry!

Mel Sanders
Cover To Cover Books

Sanctuary in Fields of Kaleidoscopic Richness
An Introduction by Dennis McBride

Ghost Town is back, courtesy of Chris and Toni, and all were invited to the party, the one we all want and need to be invited to. It's sweet, smart as hell, and tells the truth about the other real side of the tracks in Lake Wobegone. It passes the elevator test: I wouldn't mind being stuck in one if I had a copy of this anthology with me. It is a beautifully alive blast furnace of creation that releases the imagination's white sails from the stone steel prison tower of duress we call "reality," the dark king's castle demanding the soul's unconditional surrender. It is not unique; it's just that what happens there is uniquely special wherever it happens, whenever a maverick or pregnant neuron's spark goes nova in a synaptic leap to give birth to the creative brilliance of something fresh and original. The *Ghost Town* anthology is a nova nursery where imagination is in continual intercourse with the ordinary, creating the extraordinary, which is what happens when unusual modes of thought intimately and intensely encounter unusual depth of feeling, and it is the kiss of death to the sleeping soul's homeostasis and consensus reality, and what is more urgently needed in a world that tells us daily—hourly—that what you think and feel doesn't really matter.

How delightfully devious it is then to witness the regained ownership of the self in these pages, to be reintroduced to the private property of the self in a culture obsessed with the private property of an inferior stamp. Politics aside, these poets and writers are not about stealing fire from the gods, they are merely reclaiming it, insisting that we all have as much right to it as the gods do. It is not redistributing the wealth, it is redistributing the health, and the health in *Ghost Town* is the wealth of possessing a crossbow in a world of sticks

3

and clubs.

Come in. Join this exclusive unrestricted club. The only price of admission is the sacred, unassisted, anti-authoritarian human consciousness.

The poetry in *Ghost Town*, like poetry in general, does something that is unique in experience—and it's not just that poets and writers aren't usually on the payroll, though that helps. It feels more like a kind of patriotism around pirate's treasure—together with a sweetness of subversive camaraderie from artists tired of being used by the culture for target practice, and especially because of the ecstatic sense of wellbeing that sweeps over you periodically when they find that perfect combination of words. It feels at times like a jazz opera, the gravity of blues music mixing with the buoyant levity of the Beatles—it's that sweet spot in the universe you run into occasionally in jobs or relationships or dinners or bed.

I love it when poetry and satire, reverence and irreverence, hold hands, especially in a dangerously agile poetry that isn't rigidly preoccupied with the esthetics of poetic etiquette but with language as a vector of truth. Whatever the soul is, one of its dominant symptoms, after the onset of puberty, seems to be suffocation and the attendant desire to just exhale, to pay a pagan tribute to the roly-poly pursuit of pleasure and cross pollinate freedom's sustained pursuit of idleness amid the swirling tsunami of personal experience. It pulls the heavy oars of poetry out of the heavy atmosphere of the university and employs it in the experiences of the heart, the human object of the verb.

Ghost Town Poetry is the kind of book you read because its writers have supported some aspect of the truth with their recalcitrant imagination's ability to subvert Science and Philosophy and Religion's desire to provide the false assurance that there are adequate responses to any aspect of the human condition. This book contains the kind of writing you read just to be restored, to indulge in that free "press card pass" from the universe that writers can possess. If there is a lack of sympathy for anything in this anthology it is for the stoic, the unseeing, the unfeeling, the uncaring.

You come away with a renewed appreciation of the clean nobility and dignity of the motive force in the act of art, the attempt to put our cave painting story on the wall while reintroducing the world's importance as an antidote to a mankind that has become malignant with brutal competition, numbing billions, and a diversity tragically bordering on disease. It's as though even being at the heart of a nuclear winter with life being extinguished there remains something miraculous, and undeniable "yes" buried somewhere inside the bleakness, that contains the odd and most contradictory gift of both "excitement" and "sanctuary" in a mixture where both can continually change uniforms, like physics' mysterious "wave" and "particle," in fields of kaleidoscopic richness that suggest endless possibilities no one has ever seen before: what everyone is looking for, what can only be called "rescue." This writing rescues by reminding the reader that poetry is about being alive, and about keeping love alive. Not the C.S. Lewis kind of love, but the blood red embodied kind. The kind that turns the mind and heart into combustible kindling. The kind that leaves the higher and lower chakras in shambles.

This work is alchemizing the gravity of mind into the levity which leads it away from a fundamentalist's sense and toward a fundamentally desirable sense. It is a high karate mental yoga retraining the mind without the artificial feel of intentional manufacture, but rather as though a mental dowser is being used to locate occult hidden pools of delight and surprise, alternately a mad and very merry tea party where the real, unreal, and surreal are reintroduced to each other. It is electroshock to the left hemisphere, reason's reason in a rinse and spin cycle amid serious flirtation with fun, where the possibility of rescue always feels imminent. Alice has returned to the Looking Glass again with poetry that "heals the wounds inflicted by reason," and a kind of meta-coherence form begins to develop into a gradually increasing clarity like a photographic image evolving into sharpness as it lays in solution. The images emerge into connected fragments of experience quilting themselves into a recurring, recognizable truth that becomes the familiar connective tissue of living.

This anthology keeps the eye on this difficult game of life, and it's keeping an accurate score. It is like a repeating knife thrust slicing through the stage backdrop to give us a look at what lies behind. No kitsch here, no denial—there is neither a heroic place to land nor an attempt to placate with seductive nihilism. The touching and somewhat hidden strength of compassion that compels this work resides in the knowledge that none of us are superhuman enough to avoid the need for our own brand of kitsch which leaves that inviting back door to humanity open.

Bet you can't miss finding yourself somewhere in this book. If you can, put it down and go back to your *Sports Illustrated*.

POEMS

Roll Over, Beethoven

This is rock and roll. We should not be conservative and we should not be safe. ~ Cyndi Lauper

What if I set up a sound track of my life
on the *i*Pod, choosing a song, a theme
for every crucial scene, notable speech, realization?

For the moment I knew I could leave my marriage
is "Night on Bald Mountain" too obvious?

For clichés of bad faith adult behavior (example:
affair with married father of young children),
maybe something strident from *Carmen*?

Or should it all be doo-wop, R&B, rockabilly?
Because every song I heard in high school lives
inside my body. Inside, maybe, every cell.

'55-'56: Transistor radios! You could carry
the music! You could take it to the beach!

Even now, when memory bites us all, every note
every word is instantly available, total recall
shooting through me like adrenaline:

Bo Diddley/Fats Domino/Etta James/Elvis
– and Brenda Lee, who was younger than me.

I don't have those clothes anymore, but if I did –
I'd put them on and dance all night in Mickey's basement.

Elizabeth Archers

Places Remembered Before Birth

My grandmother recognized our new house
the first time she came in with my grandfather,
saying, "I've been here before" over and over,
her eyes eager for each room; knowing
the place she couldn't have been before;
my Dad shaking his head.
But then she forgot how to speak,
and never loved us again, going silent into death,
a long dream without losses.
I live at the edge of forgiveness
(in a snug, thatched cottage of mistrust),
stacked fieldstone in a slow tumble
down moss and lichen-green hillsides;
an old longing for someone, something,
somewhere deeper and further away.
The list of my enemies gets shorter
as I age into the calm boredom
of herders, flocks all in their pens.

I knew the land would fall this way, somehow,
but don't remember knowing,
and get impatient for sleep
to flee memory and release again
into dreams of forgetting
what has been lost, or will be.

Lana Ayers

Saturday Evening, Mid 1960s

My father is watering
the small, square lawn
in front of our brick-faced
ranch home, shingled
with asbestos siding.

He holds his thumb
over the garden hose nozzle
a certain way so that
the steady stream is magically
transformed to a fine spray.

I watch from the screen door,
my fingers troubling
a tiny defect in the weave,
working it into a full-fledged
hole insects will infiltrate.

I have a summer cold, so my mother
has forbidden me from going outside,
even though it's so mild my father wears
only his white sleeveless undershirt
and cotton red plaid shorts.

There's a pale rainbow in the hose mist.
I want to call out to my father
so he can see it too,
but I know he wouldn't hear me
over the rush of the liquid,

11

over the cars shushing by in the street,
over the song he's surely humming.
He won't be able to hear me
for years, and by then,
it will be too late.

Melinda Bell

Young Girls Like Me

You'd stand at Grandma's sink
washing dishes slowly,
sun threading your red hair.
I'd see you from the living room
where I lay on the floor, rolling,
listening to 45's
setting the arm over and over ~
"Your Cheatin' Heart"
"La Vie en Rose."

At bedtime you'd read me a chapter
from books with worn spines, where
> Young girls like me were brave
> and rode horses. We knew
> how to catch the brass ring.
> Our mothers loved us.

You'd leave too soon
after only a chapter or two
turn out the light. I'd sing
rocking my head
scratch my thigh red.
In my bed

I would be pretty and blond
marching on ship decks
with my silver baton
and always be chosen
to sing for the men.

Once, breathing fast
I stumbled down Grandma's dark stairs
climbed up into your bed
surprised that your back was so cold.
When will the baby come?
I wanted to ask
but already knew: soon.
> *The bull in the pasture had chased me again!*
> *chased me into the dark shed*
> *the one I always found in the nick of time*
> *and still, still, it tried to get in.*

Kristin Berger

Desire Path II

Sometimes we need half-sleep
to set all the raw assumptions
made about our lives aside –

the sheet saddling the hip
a threadbare gesture

let the hand stray

unhinge and take
with care each divine fold

of doubt

day-dreams just now
clear their throats,
know enough
to keep to themselves

like purring things in the dark.

Previously published in *The Blue Hour*, February 2013.

April Bullard

Guardian of Forgotten Souls

I am one of the Guardians of Forgotten Souls,
A watchdog of Death that tallies and tolls.
Born from the energy of discarded lives,
Bound to proclaim their unhallowed demise,
Until they are found, and in sacred ground lie,
Or their last drop of kindred bloodline dies.
Discharged to patrol a crumbling fortress,
Once a gleaming, seemingly charitable hostess.
Built to so cleanly segregate and contain,
With iron barred windows, doors locked, and gates chained,
Those whose feeble frames and skewed brains
Were more than their families could bear or sustain.

Until they succumbed to lingering ills,
Or their addled minds failed from anguish and pills,
Those deformed, or simply unable to reason,
Or confounded from the march of seasons,
Were housed in sterile, pale walls and held captive,

Not to disrupt the lives of those able and active,

Their unclaimed corpses were efficiently burned,
Remnant ashes collected, and sealed in urns.
Forms properly filled out, and papers filed,
Each canister numbered and neatly stockpiled,
In a shelf-lined room beneath the foundation,
Locked to maintain their death as salvation.

Many years passed, and the metal jars mounted,
The basement room full, over three thousand counted.
Disregarded, dismissed, memories lost in the gloom,
That burial chamber now a dungeonous tomb.
With emotional strength, not corporeal form,
I must make manifest that blasphemous dorm.

All the cast aside, unmourned souls resonate,
And my ghostly, spiritual powers grow great.
With the ferocious fury of the unjustly damned,
Fulfilling my duty, a door will be slammed.
I make the pounding, pleading of souls sealed in tin
Echo in each footfall of those passing within.

I whisper through windowsills, leave frost on the panes.
Shed tears down the walls, the paint blisters, and stains.
I grow in your shadow, monstrous shapes dance and bend,
Then I breathe down your neck, every hair stands on end.
My frigid finger that traces your spine
Beckons you to discover those souls confined.

I am one of the Guardians of Forgotten Souls,
A watchdog of Death that tallies and tolls.
Born from the energy of discarded lives,

Bound to proclaim their unhallowed demise,
Until they are found, and in sacred ground lie,
Or their last drop of kindred bloodline dies.

Back in the spring of 2011, the news headline "Room of Unclaimed Souls" caught my attention. The Oregon State Hospital's room of 3500 copper canisters of forgotten and unclaimed patient remains lead to my poem "Guardian of Forgotten Souls." I was so excited, I created the Ghost Town Poetry Challenge October 2011 to encourage fellow writers to participate, and submitted the poem for publication. My poem was published in parABnormal Digest #2, Sept 2011 from Sam's Dot Publishing and I performed the piece at the Ghost Town Poetry Open Mic in October 2011. The Ghost Town Poetry Open Mic offered a unique gathering of striving authors and artists, where I could perform and hone my work towards my goal of publication.

Tiffany Burba-Schramm

Where Sunflowers Go To Die

Nathan,

I found the sunflowers.
They are in a community garden
across the street from my old high school.

I saw them
some are holding on,
still erect with large blooms.

Some droop just slightly.
Water might help raise their heads.

Some have petals missing,
scattered below on the weeded earth.

One giant head is brown and dead,
just left there to decompose

The afternoon sky is muggy.
The air is hot.

The yellow and brown and green colors
flash before my camera lens.

I snap feverishly.
My daughter yells, "Mom, we need to go!"

I walk slowly towards my car.
Sadness swirls like a dust storm around my head.
The dust creates tightness in my throat.

I know where the sunflowers go to die.
Click click click before they run out of time.

Previously published in the 2013 chapbook *Sunflower Blues*.

Sheryl Clough

Virgin Under Glass

The Wee House of Malin is a natural cave in a rocky hillside at Malin Head, Ireland. Just outside the cave is a glassed-in Blessed Virgin statue, originally standing in the school on Inishtrahull, but relocated to the mainland when that island was abandoned.

When the Virgin of Malin looks at her feet, she sees candles, prayers on yellowed paper, flowers fresh and dead, and shells from the North Atlantic shore.
When I look at my feet, I see dirt, squashed bugs, chipped

lacquer, and a blackberry vine from the field, clinging
like a lover newly discarded.

She gazes out, the Virgin statue, from behind her Plexiglas
window. No worries over bugs, vines or windstorms — just
freedom to bask in devotions from summer pilgrims.

That adulation must feel great. I'll never know, being a mere
digger on the shore, filling my pockets with tide-polished
agates, my cheeks beaten raw by the North Wind.

The Virgin cannot know the wind, that holy siren forcing up
the collar on my jacket, rocking fishing boats at anchor,
leaving her serene behind her screen, and quiet.

Ed Coletti

Perhaps Not Yet

Frank may not admit it,
but he actually enjoys dithering,
searching about for words that aren't there
for him and then swimming about in a familiar
confusion a vast ocean he claims to know little about
for he after all is neither oceanographer nor computer,
and, were it not for this strangely pleasant feeling
like a privileged aching deep in marrow, Frank
might permit himself to be more frightened
of his brain than of his bodily insults, and
he would sink like a depressing anchor
into regions of the sea he cannot feel.

Joyce Colson

In the Winter of Life

In the winter of life,
The fading sunset of the experience,
The lingering awareness of falling leaves,
The slowing warmth of summer wind,
The whisper of the heart that grows older,
There is but one lingering consolation:
Wisdom has replaced our foolishness.

Previously published in the chapbook *The River's Flow*.

Brittney Corrigan

What They Won't See

Finally, after unspectacular years in the windows
of our small string of homes, our night blooming cereus
is budding. A bud the size of an egg, wrapped in long,
purpled tendrils muzzling forward to the tip, perched
at the end of a thick, curving stalk. It is the last week
of June in a summer slow to arrive, cast in cloud cover
and rain after rain. We are tired—a week of children
coughing in their sleep, of night terrors and moving
from their beds into ours. But we will stay up to see it open,
perhaps tonight, perhaps tomorrow, watch the tendrils
peel back to reveal feathery white petals, a bird of a blossom
spreading its full, fragrant body forward into the dark.

We don't want to miss it. But also today, I am thinking
of what our dead are missing. What they won't see.
Their deaths are still close, near enough that our children
remember them with equal parts confusion and longing.

Sometimes I can accept that they are gone. But not the morning
we wake to find our son has grown taller overnight. Not the day
my husband arrives home from a long weekend trip to remark
that our daughter is bigger. Her body fills up more space,
her toes reach out farther into the room. Not the times
when these children unfurl with their growing, so quickly
you can almost see their young arms lengthening toward the sky.
And I think, how can they be sleeping, our dead? *Wake up.*
Be here to see this. You can't miss this flowering, this bloom.

Previously published in *Navigation* (The Habit of Rainy Nights Press,
2012).

Michael Daley

The Death of the Sparrow Hawk

I stood at the kitchen window.
A glass of water, then wade
The uncut grass with the dog,
But I heard a swarm of goldfinches,

A ruined choir in millet and corn,
Whoosh of butter yellow fans,
The kestrel rang through the yard,
Swooped above the rhodie.

A secret loosening of bones in the skull,
Muscles along my hips —
Hungry little sparrow hawk,
Sags the rippled power line.

In tall grass I toss a ball
The dog forgets,

Blue like nothing,
Fire pit pinched the willow.

Her feathertip curves away from maples,
Their scree-eak winds her in circles
Past the two balds—wing-spins twice hers,
Flap like shook flannel,

Not a tree in the pasture for rest,
They parry her dash to and fro,
Faithful as tango partners,
Pass above the neighbors' roan—

The dog yips for a toss—
Pass round a hemlock,
When now three eagles
Tamper with her orbit,

Deprive her of purchase.
Loud screeks and their arcs
Or bless us all, gyres
Narrow, not widening, for the kill.

The sparrow hawk's wing
Torn at the sky,
Plumb to thorn
By the ball, chewed blue neon.

Eileen Davis Elliott

Cats' Head Biscuits

no bread in the tin box
the last slices went to school lunch lard sandwiches
but, pork chops already done
fried crisp with brown drippings in the pan

biscuits the answer
pull down the blue bowl
stir up a white blizzard
coffee cups of flour
a heaping soupspoon of calumet
salt pour duration of automatic knowledge
nose tickles in the flour cloud

—throw a little flour into the pork chop pan
make a roux—

cut in some lard with two slashing forks
a practiced, honed art
stir in the clabber milk
crocked on the porch

—what we don't use, the pigs will
but we win every time
remember the chops warming over the boiler—

swiped cast iron griddle
with rag from lard crock on the shelf
plop dough in big, big spoonsful
eight white mountains on the black iron

tractor chugs, puffs into the dooryard
disc blades rattling over worn-out gravel

slide the dough into the heavy-doored oven
with luck, biscuits will puff up
big as cats' heads
browned to perfection

Kathleen Flenniken

NEWS ITEM

"New research suggests we have a fixed reservoir of self-restraint."

This is why at the end of the day
you smuggle bowls of ice cream to the TV

Or put another way
when you pushed your plate aside
and hunger kneaded your gut for months
this is why you crammed the closet with new clothes
and emerged from your diving bell
in a breathless hotel room
why you let the coat fall from your shoulders

That manic week
when you ironed every shirt and tablecloth
why you couldn't keep up with the grief

Last night sirens passed close
this morning the airwaves crash and moil

and your mail is flooded with catalogs

This is why you've staged your house like a catalog
why you can't bear to open the bills
why streets are jammed with luxury cars
and panhandlers
and your country is at war

Previously published in *Tar River Poetry*, Spring 2012.

NOVEMBER TRITINA

November is a necklace of daytime headlights
crossing the floating bridge. Silk
breast of a winter wren, scarf tied loosely at the neck. It's the
sun

or more correctly, its lack. No, you're my sun,
parsing the fog, light
spun and suspended in a web. November is a grey silk

suit, white shirt, dark silk
tie with a wine stain, Sun-
day coat, all in a pile, headlight

beams through a scrim and a distant horn. Light head, silky
breath, sun going down.

Previously published in *Alaska Quarterly Review*, Spring/Summer 2012.

Daniel Gilchrist

Don't Be

Turning point
point of no return
last chance
chance not taken
moment gone
gone with the consensus
just because
because you're one of the sheep
Don't be

Previously published in the chapbook *Frog Tongue* (Small Poetry Press, 1995).

Rob Gourley

Taking Solace in Dante
(*Inferno* Canto XXX, 18-21)

Four lines concerning Hekuba in Thrace ...

> *e del suo Polidoro in su la riva*
> *del mar si fu la dolorosa accorta,*
> *forsennata latrò sì come cane;*
> *tanto il dolor le fé la mente torta –*

remind me of the Japanese in harm's way, Sendai
Earthquake/Tsunami, subsequent Fukushima
nuclear catastrophe, and now armored assault
on Syrian city neighborhoods by Syrian Army!

Finding her last son's lifeless shape wash'd up onshore,
  she collapsed with sorrow on that sandy spot
and like an abandon'd sheepdog, whimpered there all night,
his murder had left her so broken and distraught.

Johnna Gurgel

Pull My Train in Now

I'll be ready – Lord so ready
When my train pulls in. I'm
Waiting with my bags packed
And I've got loved ones said
Goodbye – Lord I'm ready. Pull
My train in.
I'm waiting ready down on
The station tracks listening for
The rocks to shake from that
Thunderous echoing quake. I'm
Waiting ready to hear that sound –
Yes, anytime now.
I'm wanting gone; I want the
Life below and back to be covered
In the smokestack black chugging
Chugging chugging down the
Final track. Take me to the beloved town.
I'm singing the calling sound
Lord I'm ready waiting; any day now.
Pull my train in and let me feel
The giving sound. Yes God, I am
Ready now.

Miles Hewitt

Poem on a Napkin

Folded twice on a booth in the back of the Jantzen Beach Denny's
there is a napkin, creased like a tapestry depicting arts of war and
conquest. The floral pattern ensnaring the edge represents the
Babylonian Hanging Gardens. Nearby a girl in a prom dress
practices getting her feelings hurt: blush, pout, her long black hair
shining dully like the River Styx. Unattended, her phone vibrates
three times. The background image flashes: LIVE♥LAUGH♥LOVE.
Size twelve Times New Roman, fuchsia like her lips.
O, to be anywhere else, anytime else!
On the jukebox Ella Fitzgerald sounds like floodwater, like an ocean
reciting its tide. The Columbia River is just down the road, proving
there are times you cannot avoid the fishes. I am so fucking tired of
human sensitivity. Why can't we all be white stale patient plodding
napkins, apolitical, silent? I would sit in Denny's and eavesdrop and
clean up their messes.

David Hill

Sunrise

The colors of a Balkan city sunrise –
Sulfuric orange and exhaust-fume blue –
Envelop proletarian apartments
And bathe the blinking eyes of me and you.
They set ablaze the gray unblooming treetops,
The old red setter bounding round the park,
And kiss the windows of the Party palace:
A hundred torches burning through the dark.

The system that produced this scene is dead now,
A system set to last a thousand years;

Where all men bore the flame of common struggle
And set aside possessions and careers.
Where work was for the simple joy of working,
And no one was rewarded for their skill,
And economic surplus was invested
In monuments to one great common will.

And who's to say the thought was so outlandish,
When all around us, not so far away,
The pious come together in their orders,
To labor and to suffer and to pray?
And who will disagree that monks and abbots
Who shelter from the world and its events
To tend their ideologies and gardens
Are communist, in the profoundest sense?

The icon-laden church that rises proudly
Above the lowly cloisters of the meek;
The uniform philosophy that stifles,
The rations, the rewards you must not seek;
It seems to work so well when people choose it,
And when their numbers are extremely small –
Why wasn't it successful on a large scale,
And was the structure always bound to fall?

I do not know the algorithmic function,
The Darwinist selection that applies,
That rakes through these experimental communes
And picks them out according to their size.
I know that recent history's been kinder
To government as picked by people's vote –
The worst known type, except for all the others,
According to that old Churchillian quote.

There's beauty in the smallest thing of nature,
And that includes the things our race creates.
There's some internal logic to our projects,
Our pyramids and palaces and states.
There's some renewal heaving through our concrete,
Behind the words of president and priest –
So let me hold your hands that hold my heartstrings,
And let us share the sunrise in the east.

Rainy Knight

Do You Speak English?

In Amsterdam, the man at the hostel counter nods and says,
Yes, I do
In Luxembourg, the man at that hostel counter, smiles and
Says, yes
In Paris, the woman looks slightly perplexed, but says, a little
In Stuttgart, the woman says, of course
In Zurich, the man says: as you wish and then, when I offer
Euros for post cards, he says: Only Swiss francs here –
We are not part of the European Union, or the UN!

In Florence, the woman at the hostel counter says:
I will do my best…
In Genoa, the woman at the hostel counter speaks first,
        in English
So I do not ask
In Barcelona, the boys at the hostel counter speak English
With barely traces of accent,
Even though they are from Norway and Hungary

Every time I get lost (which is often, in train stations and in

The bus systems) I ask: Do you speak English?
Because that is a Rick Steves tip I believe valuable

Luckily I find many who can, only a few who cannot
Or as in Paris, will not for their own petty reasons

Kudos to Natasha, a Russian woman who goes out of
Her way to help me find my hostel, gestures & smiles
No language to join our conversation
It is in Florence and she has only the hostel address
I show her

She recruits an Italian boy who speaks English to direct
Me where to go then walks with me for miles
When we find the road in, it is uphill and long
She flags down a couple from Eastern Europe,
Who offer to drive me the rest of the way

When I offer Euros for her trouble, she shakes
Her head 'no', then hugs me, kisses my cheek
And walks away
Natasha speaks no English, but she communicates
Very well…

Christi Krug

On the Path

Here it is:
a robin's eggshell
telling the story of a flight
before it happened.
There was a rocking, a splitting

I cracked open.

Now it comes:
the placing of a god-house
into my hand.

I fear this eggskin may crumble,
heaven may break.
Still I learn to walk
hand outstretched,
preserving the frail and unnested,

the blue inside the blue of me
open to the air
healing the seam of blood
within the creamy white.

See: you can!
Holding sky and wonder,
sing and carry
the long, blue, fragile cup of your life.

Jake Loranger

A Story About Poetry

Poetry, simply a deity, it flows through
you and me,
slashes through the crowd like a guillotine.
When nothing offers an escape or expression,
hopefully you remember me and my poetry,
but specifically my fluidity, lucidity,
serenity: a trinity.

31

Sorry if I'm blabbering,
it's just the crowd is staggering,
rhyming without trying is a very easy thing.
I'd end with formalities, but there's no need,
we're all just simple entities,
human beings, fragile things,
and when you see you can see through me,
you'll be surprised to see my insanity.

Lori Loranger

The Cool Mom

I listen to you honey,
and I'm thinking
I used to BE you,
only I took more drugs,
had more sex,
and made more bad decisions
While still excelling by superficial standards.
Other parents display
shock and outrage
to discover that I will give you
the benefit of my experience
through direct truth.

What method should I use –
indirect lies?

I am derisively chided
for "trying to be the cool Mom" –
Well, I guess that's half right;

but I'm not trying –
I really am just
        that
          cool.

Zoe Loranger

Collections

You keep cups of tears I've cried
To remind you of the demons you carry.
To act as angels of your yesterday
To keep you from repeated wrongs
So for you I collect

A dialect of broken words
bent passages
a guide to mishaps and mayhem.

Distractions from your losses;

You are a collection
of thought processes and pauses
A puzzle for a level-head
A lock made for a better convict
Growing up in a world of conflict
Because no man could grasp your concepts

Pull me apart and talk me through the process
And I'll cry for you some beautiful tears
And you'll keep them
so you don't forget
I'll make sure to collect

Jack Lorts

Ephram Pratt Speaks in the Language of Seals

He lived near the sea
and his days were filled

conversing softly with
deceased mermaids;

but from them
he learned

the language of seals,
the grunts, the whistles,

the body language,
the subtle eye movements.

The cottage on the cape
was filled with ancestors,
peopled with tiny clones
of whoever lived there.

Only in the shadows
did he allow himself to speak

the language he knew so well,
he loved so insanely.

Why should he not speak
with seals?

The language known by poets

since time began.

Previously published in *Fault Lines*, 2012.

Peter Ludwin

Breakfast in Baja
for Russell Salamon

Restaurant Jalisco, the sign read,
    a two-room adobe hovel
        sticking up like a wart

from the desert floor. *Noooo,*
    you said, *it's too funky,*
        we'll get something nobody's got a cure for,

but we went in anyway
    to the little patio
        with its lone table covered with sand,
which the old man's wife
    swept away with her hand
        before she took our order.

You didn't want anything
    but she misunderstood
        and brought out two plates

of eggs and beans and tortillas,
    which we had to eat or insult them
        and slink away like whipped dogs,

and you grudgingly conceded how good it was
    while she kept bringing more plates

of tortillas without us saying a word,

and avocados, and chickens ran by
    from the garden
        and three kids kept trying

to get the radio to work
    by beating on it with a hammer,
        and the old man

went about his chores
    hauling buckets of water back and forth,
        the two meals coming to about $1.75.

Do you remember, my friend, how that
    breakfast lasted all the way to San Felipe,
        where the pelicans flocked to greet us?

Previously published in *The Midwest Quarterly* (Winter 1999) and *Rumors of Fallible Gods* (Presa Press, 2010).

M

Don't Ask Don't Tell

This pleasant dental hygienist with her fingers
in my mouth asks *So do you have any*
children? and I want to tell her that her
elbows rising on either side of my head
look like griffin wings, for some strange
reason, those mythical creatures with a duty
to protect what's priceless, along with the power
to transport me back to that gynecologist's office

thirty years ago, the fifth I'd consulted, his pink
consent form asking *Does your husband agree*
to your sterilization? and to the signature I'd forged
on the paperwork just as I had as a girl of fourteen
in need of parental permission to watch a sex-ed film
that promised all the answers to whatever
marvels and misconceptions men keep hidden
in their pants pockets, but never delivered,
before the parade of friend after friend came rolling
through, handing me their babies to cradle, hopeful
one perfect embrace could induce
in me the birth of want and the opening of a door
to my mother, whose grandchild balloon
I'd popped one afternoon, her face sick, her hands
extending a new white terrycloth robe
that said if total disarmament was out
of the question, at least we could call a cease-fire
over my belly that would never carry more than a couple
of stitches through my umbilicus, and all those predictions
of regret, inaccurate as Portland forecasts that fail
to include one of our fifty-seven varieties
of rain. But it's impolite to talk with your mouth
full. I shake my head from side to side instead,
her sympathetic fingers still in the dark.

Previously published in *On The Issues Magazine*, Winter 2013.

David Madgalene

Ghost Whores

You see that house over there?
It used to be called the Osaka.
It was a massage parlor,
but they busted it for prostitution.
That was a couple years ago,
and they haven't been able
        to rent it since.
        You know why?
They say it's because
the place is haunted by
the ghosts of the whores
who used to work there.
You may think it sounds fun,
but believe me, you don't want
to be standing there and get
sucked-off by something
you can't see what it is,
if you know what I mean,
or you might just be lying
there minding your own
business, and the next thing
you know you've got
Casper the Friendly Ho
bouncing up and down
on your dick. And the
scariest thing of all?
You open up your
wallet, and you find
twenty dollars gone!

Jim Martin

Quiet

Quiet,
at peace with the world,
trees: their trunks, bathed
in the soft texture of spring grasses,
hold this hill in place
and dream their gentle dreams.

Close, I am at peace;
at peace with them,
and their world,
and with the knowledge that
cells and tissues
in my brain,
crafted by millennia,
see the trees
and think this thought.

Thoughts like these go not quiet
into a world of thinkers
and believers,
those who veil deep within them
the fear that we are
of this Earth;
That what we see,
and feel,
and think,
has been felt
by others, nearly like us,
long, long ago.

Mr. Mu, Strict Physics

When Mr. Mu doesn't have anything else to do
he wonders about the strict physics
of his illusion dreaming,
and then the dream within the dream
of the dreamerless machine, how all that pencils out,
the careworn part, to care that much.
Pink hollyhocks climb their clockworks,
someone's shouting at someone else on the corner,
he can smell the freebased deep fry
from out the Pump & Munch roof vents,
and fights back a drool. Four crows
go at it like a talk show in a 2-story cherry
giving itself over to a galactic breeze
in some crazy summer harmony his brain can't contain.
No one's can, not even Emily Dickinson's.
That's what the heart's for, if it doesn't break first.
His neighbor's giant wind chimes *bong bung*
bong on a soundtrack THX can't touch.
When he gets like this he sees fractals
behind his eyes. Mu.
His mu, your mu, this mu, our mu.
The atoms whirled up and said I am Mr. Mu,
who mused on that until he saw through it,
staring at the threadbare Happy Face of care.
Tears what are tears he sighed to his no one there.

David Matthews

More Young Than Yesterday

How unadorned this day —
Trees pencil drawn, gray,
bare wintered limbs
in crisscross weave form
a stark abstraction worn
against the silvered sky.

The café is warm and bright
where I come with time to pass
before the evening's
film festival offering.

The impossibly young barista shyly explains
it is only her third day
when she has to ask a coworker
if they serve decaf americano —

more young than yesterday,
innocent as comb
in a dormitory of bald monks.

Dennis McBride

Birds in Search of a Poem

When the galaxy of Vaux Swifts
returns to fill the Anchorage evening sky
with their swift black constellations,
this is not the poem.
But have you seen them!
I mean the million birds expanding and contracting
for real, on the edge of chaos,
right up there above you,
neck-bending, head-looking-up real
and then also in the sky of the mind —
the mind that knows only the small facts of migration,
where they are from, where they are going.
The mind that is reduced to the mud-star wonder of it.
It! This hundred thousand million birds
shooting and swirling and darting
above the giant grade school chimney
awaiting the soft signal of dusk to descend into it
like a million black sky rabbits disappearing
back into the magician's large stone hat.
This is not the poem.
But when the last five become the last one.
When the inscrutable instruction
swallows the last Swift into the giant mouth.
When the great stone chimney
is silent and still.
This is the poem.

The Rats

They make no mistakes
because they don't know how

The small shiny innocent spies
cough and hiccup and fart,
scurry dimly down dark hidden caverns
with messages of the eternal secret.
They are small frightened cows without bliss
but know they are deserving
and will not be intimidated.

They are religious little rodents
who love no one but turn darkness
into their light

and when they stumble over a fork
lying on the dark night's kitchen floor
god equates it with the holocaust

They watch us quietly from ceilings and cellars,
see the garbage rise and spill over,
know there are too many of us to last like this.

They love the sun but do not trust it
and when it rains the holy whiskers twitch
and they smell the scent of their women
and bring them spiders like flowers

Mike G

Great Tribulation

Merry Go Muse floating in the zeitgeist,
In childhood's glossolalian ecstasy,
In uncanny interludes between blooms.
Always a pallbearer, never a corpse,
Unmarked helicopters singing within,
Spinning addiction to fish blood on hook.
So you're the property of Jesus now,
Fingerpainting ghosts with hand grenades,
And the council you keep is silent.
Let's meet by the dolphin and the cross,
Rip out the System's rotten teeth.
Put on the green wig and kiss me.
See those stars in my head? Make a wish,
Win the brain's great tribulation,
Live! Spread wings over New Jerusalem.

A. Molotkov

The Engineer of My Dreams

the engineer of my dreams
leaves work early
she has other things to do
other minds to stir

for the rest of the night
my dreams are unattended
unreliable
they don't follow the rules
like a drunken sailor

overnight
in an imaginary port

Borders

a river
crosses a border
without a visa

I am tired
and yet my mind jumps out of bed
and sings

listen, Butterfly!

be careful
take good care of your wings
the world has rough edges
dangerous borders
tall buildings
burning airplanes

Russell Munroe

OLY

Olympia is waking up.
I can see it in their eyes.
I can see it in the way they walk,
Yawning at the sky.
Above the Urban Onion,
An elderly man in pajamas

Dances with his cat
And, after buttered wheat toast and jam
He puts on his favorite hat.
A few floors up the Oly PD
Studies the subcultures of Sylvester Park.
Face seeks respite from an abscess tooth in the gazebo.
"The pain, the pain," he says,
"…must be baptized like a spark."
Leilani sees her first morning at her new pad.

Angeline Nguyen

Remembering Ophelia

I stood with one foot on dry land
The other tasting the water
Where they say a good girl had drowned
Bound cruelly to the man-made weight
Despair.

Through osmosis, or some other
Equally magical process,
The liquid memories became
Tame and flowed through my five toes and
Senses.

Time danced and contortioned itself
Until Past overlaid Present
And I could see the girl walk by
My side, solid as convictions
And Trust.

Freshly-cut flowers on the bank

Atone for the ones she carried
Until they left her arms and wound
'Round her body, gently twisting
Like Truth.

They fell as she waded, then sank
Into the darkness of the brook.
Although I knew she was not there,
Care stretched out my hand as though it
Could help.

I imagined that her sorrow
Conquered instinct for survival
So that when gravity called her
Closer to Earth's persuasive core
She smiled.

The sun refused not to shine and
Wind rippled the water's surface
Where whispers lingered in Surround
Sound as flesh resolved water and
Goodbye.

Maggie O'Mara

Ghosts of Siberia

Through white stillness
your silent footsteps fall
as I track you across
the snow covered wastes

Your forest realm

smaller than it once was
I wonder...
are you still there
am I tracking you
in this world of frozen wooden columns
or a shadow—an impression
left behind

Do I see you...?
your stripes blend—fade into
the dark cold forest
Do I see you...?
Savage king striding alone
Do I see you...?
Graceful Queen—children trailing
in court

Silent forest—silent footfalls
Ghosts in the frozen wastes
soundless shadows
majestic, regal, precious
in your feline glory
your presence a gift
squandered, desecrated, dishonored
I see you now
my brothers, my sisters
I watch your progress
you ascend to the stars
from this poorer plane
the world pales
at your passing

Jenney Pauer

Snapshot of Helen of Troy

I found a picture of you with Big Uncle and you
are smiling and your eyes look kind,
and I consider how the random stranger who is
passing you in the background is caught, forever,
admiring you. And I remember how, as a little girl,
I took it for granted that you would always create
this effect, like some human equivalent of a capillary
wave, a ripple in a pond, following its limited boundary,
while shaping the ambiguous laws of physical desire.

I remember how your Chanel scent lifted with the loose
strands of your black hair, and how the exotic oval of your
face remained inscrutable as deferential men held the
door for you in public places, but I mostly remember
your offhand comment, years later, when I was struggling
through my adolescence, of how your female boss tried
to pimp you out to her male supervisors at Westinghouse,
and then fired you when you refused to be the
in-house Asian whore.

I think about all the petty women who envied you, who
resented your thin body and lovely curves, who saw you
when you were playing Korean cute and mistook your life for
a gum drop colored carnival ride. I wonder what they would
have thought if they could have seen the three of us living in
the studio apartment with the cockroaches and the leering
neighbors. If they had known how afraid you were to have a
boyfriend because you were already so well aware of how
men could hurt little girls. What would it have done to them
to realize that Helen of Troy doesn't win?

After your heart attack, I visited you and took another picture. In this one, you smile like a grim debutante. Your face is spotted and oily. Your hair is coarse and cut short like a man's. The photograph doesn't show it, but your hands are scaly from psoriasis. You live in your car and show up on my sisters' doorsteps unannounced.

I held your claws in mine and braved the flaking skin and sores. To my shame, I hesitated after you asked me if I loved you. It was only for a second, but it was enough.

Jennifer Pratt-Walter

Target

for Malala Yousafzai

If you wear hate on your head
or draped over your shoulders
long enough, it turns into
a gun.

The girl had lips
soon to be kissable,
a curious mind blooming below
the pale flag of a headscarf,
a voice like clean light linen,
eyes dark as the night
of new moon,
soul of a slender new visionary,

until hate
changed her lips and eyes into
a target,

her brain a home
for bullets—
but true vision remained
as girl-blood seeped across
light blue linen.

Sidra Grace Quinn

Standing in for Love
With deep gratitude to the forgotten poet who inspired this poem.

To feel grief not your own
you must first wipe the steam
from the back window
of your parents' car

as your sister
and Johnny Barlow
scramble into his pink
Dodge Dart.

You watch as they drive off
and imagine them speeding
onto the back road,
the one with pot holes as large as lakes;
Gravel hitting the underside
of the car like music.

You see your sister's hand
on Johnny Barlow's knee
and the peek-a-boo
of teeth between
her coral lips.

You smell exhaust fumes,
sweat, melting hairspray
and an odor
you won't recognize until
years later in the back
of some car
with a boy whose hair is as black
as Johnny's was then.

The scent of longing and lust
and what stands in for love
when it is given to a boy
with tin cans on his soul

The day you stop saying no,
because yes feels easier.

Previously published in *Cirque*.

Dan Raphael

Headrain

Is my head in the rain or the rain in my head
breathing water interrupted by drops of air
trying to give the street thought

If my head is the earth is the rest of me dark matter,
if dark matters, when light keeps flowing from my pockets,
leaking from where I must control my deposits:
every time I use my credit card I'm blinded with a
          prosperous universe
ensphering me with transparent unbreachable

Head awash with b-rain
cant remember how my head looked before it was clear cut,
before all this erosion above and below the surface

Carlos Reyes

**After Misreading The Line, Conjugations
Of The Verb "To Be"**   *for Stanley Kunitz*

Maybe I misread another line, too.

Is it the layers of lives or lies
we confront each day of our existence?

"To be" Congratulations!
You are the most powerful of verbs.

You are the substantive for liars.

With your help I can be
anything and often am
or be anyplace I want to be,

like now I am in the split and spilled boxes
and dusty cluttered storage room of my mind,

or paddling down the warm muddy surface
of the Colorado River to the Sea of Cortez.

I am in my office in front of—
I *am* a computer writing something or nothing.

As Popeye says "I am, what I am" not

who I was
in that moment and forever

when I decided to be someone else.

I stand behind that lie or truth, that life
left behind, guarding it from the light

in a fortress of round dark stones
collecting dew that encourages moss.

If the letters sent to that person
end up

in the Dead Letter Office

I will not claim them.

Kristin Roedell

My Dog and I Go Worshipping Flight

The first walk of the day when the bracken
is still damp from morning's rain,
the fence posts are footed in mud.
I bring a ball colored like the underside
of a shell or the belly of a salmon.
I throw it far and my dog runs after
until she is small as the cupped
hand shading my eyes.

She leaps, but neither crests like a whale
or makes a bell or parabola

or any algebraic curve; she jumps forward
to meet the ball the way an eagle
glides parallel to the river, talons
outstretched, grasping a pale bellied fish.
She opens her mouth and body, takes the ball
in, and only then does she acknowledge
ground, species, limitation.

This is part of the temple I build to the day,
the moment my dog disbelieves
the earth. She and I go worshipping
flight on the first walk; her ears unfurl
like sails when the bracken
is wet with rain.

Previously published in *Open Minds Quarterly*, Fall 2013.

Michael Rothenberg

May 19: Forest News

Orange butterfly wings
Pulse on the doormat

A reckless dawn
Hangs on the garden fence

Like a broken bird
There is no truth

Only an itch behind the knee
Beneath ashen leaves

63 freedomfighters
shot dead in Damascus

The squirm and twitch
of smoke in sweet rain

Previously published in *Murder* (Paper Press, 2013).

Ralph Salisbury

Like The Sun In Storm

There was a place
where the big kids let me hide, the space
too small for any of them,
between a white lilac and one
like the sun in storm
or the blood of a butchered pig
darkened by earth, and when
the game was done
and everyone else had got caught
I stayed and still stay
in the nest of the big one's willingness
to let me become
the pretend child of all of them
and the sense that the world--
despite some slaps and the occasional
crunch of knuckles against teeth
and my brother being sent to war–
could be really good.

Previously published in Like the Sun in Storm (*The Habits of Rainy Nights Press*, 2012).

Katharine Salzmann

Sex At Dawn

In the morning we make *mascarpone*
let the ridicule of butterfat lapse
into a spathic ecstasy of long
white silk. We drink as one
proteinaceous unit joined around
the idea of *tiramisu*, a coffee
so black and gritty it drags
us clear of side effects.

Cake for breakfast is what gods do
as they saturate us, soak us,
sop us up. Here we are stuck
on our gods' tines, wet and, O yes,
glistening in early side light,
anxious even to consume
and be consumed.

Erato

To call a fox out
the poet does the opposite
of what you might suppose:
snaps the pot lid off last night's broccoli
& whacks it to a fury
with a scum-stained spoon.
No sweet-talk here: She
knows he can feel it coming,
her carbonous poem, her bell,
her demon tattoo as it
peals down just under that

new slip of moon,
just under the shadow
the grass casts over itself,
between each blade
her stainless steel howl
shinks exactly toward
the thigh-wide hole
he's holed up in,
past eyes half-hung
from dope & do-gooding it
all day, right,
like a neutron caterwaul, a dead-on
stridulation, true to the track
that beelines into his suddenly
upturned ear, the fury
meant to rattle his dark envelope
and the perfect music she knows
is there.

Published online in the *Salt River Review,* Fall 2008.

Raúl Sánchez

Araucan **Goddess**

Gift in hand she arrived
fluffy black skirt and red top
brightly decked lilac hair

week after Easter purple banners
washed away the color turning lighter
flopping in the wind
like tattered prayer flags reminder

of my forfeited salvation
my own complacency.

When she walked, her cadence
reminded me of *cumbia* songs
I danced in Bogotá.

She, a dark-skinned goddess
from *Arauca*,
guiro's rhythm and *gaitas*

sound repetition moved
our feet as we got closer
her curly black hair disentangled

touched my face
at every twirl and turn
I held her right hand

with my left
ending with her back against
my chest where I could smell

her fragrance emanating
deep from her dark *mulata* skin
dark like coffee tobacco and rum

sweet as lilacs in bloom
summertime mist
a woman like her could transform

even the most humble man
not knowing what destiny

would bring I remained serene

composure lost
decided to conquer—
immerse myself

in her lilac self

Mary Slocum

Longing To Go

It was that spring renewal
Winter goin away
When the desire for leavin
Was leafin out
And the high desert
Callin coyote loud
From that place where the Ohhhs echoed
When last the sage grouse mated
At sunrise in the sagebrush
Boomin and dancing
Yellow brite flashin all around
Female's attention risin with the sun.

This spectacle, the awe of it all.
Turkey vultures lookin down from
An abandoned fire watch tower
Malheur, that place
That gets in your blood
Like the vampire's bite
Like returnin to the womb

Rain/No Rain

What can we say about rain that would not be cliché?
Still, let us try.

Perhaps rain is

like a leaking seal on an absinthe fountain, a hole worn
through the marble stand where Edgar Allen Poe sat his
glass, trying to keep the tintinnabulation of tinnitus from
driving him terribly mad.

Maybe not? Maybe that insistent, repetitious droning on and
on rain is not the rain you've experienced;

maybe your rain is

like a belly-dancer on a hot-corrugated roof, her thousand toes
wildly pattering, her shimmy shaking the bells, bells, bells on
roof-hips, the roofs sweaty and steamy for her.

Of course, I could be wrong; perhaps the temperature and
tone of that rain is too immediate for you, not titillating
enough for you.

Maybe your rain is

like a longed for lover eventually returning after months and
months without sex, so that just the scent of her or him makes
even the hard ground soft, all muddy and slippery in puddle-
anticipation.

OK, so you don't like being in a desert without an oasis
nearby; you need that quick, satisfying immersion before
another short dry spell.

Maybe your rain is

like the deluge, the monsoon, the typhoon, the god-forsaken,
soaking flood in which everything and everyone drowns
because you just can't stop rain dancing, just can't stop
drumming and drumming for more downpours, can't stop
turning your face heavenward, opening your mouth to gurgle
in your lust!

Stop, maybe your rain doesn't get that carried away; maybe

symbolically your rain is all wet, not really a dead metaphor,
just a damp one.

Leah Stenson

Head Tripping at the Chelsea Hotel

Stan, the owner, tells me I can have
Leonard Cohen's room.
Did he offer me this iconic place
because I told him I wanted a quiet space,
or does he take me for Suzanne, half-crazy,
someone who'd feed Leonard *tea and*
oranges that came all the way from China?
Or maybe he pegged me for a Janis,
who'd give Leonard *head*
on the unmade bed while
limousines wait in the street.

Who cares? Here I sit alone at the table
feasting on tea and oranges,
tuning in to Leonard's wavelength,
touching his perfect music
with my mind.

The Turquoise Bee

A flower withers in a month's time. But the turquoise bee doesn't grieve.
At the ending of an affair I will not grieve either.*

The sixth Dalai Lama,
tantric adept and Bohemian poet
adorned with jewels and blue silk robes
instead of saffron or crimson,
partied till dawn in Lhasa's brothels
and bars when he wasn't busy
pollinating some aristocratic beauty.

Renouncing his monastic vows, he
kept only his title as incarnation
of the Bodhisattva of Compassion.

Isn't love just a stop on the path
to enlightenment?

*From *The Turquoise Bee: The Love Songs of the Sixth Dalai Lama* by Fields,
Cutillo and Oda.

Under the Speed Limit

The harsh sounds of my unused
Spanish on a night when the dust hovers in the air

clouding out the more distant buildings
reminds me of all the things that fall short,

that have fallen short.
The pants I had to wear that barely touched my ankles.

The evening walk by the Willamette River
where everything was right

except I only almost loved him.
I want to be driving in a clear-aired desert

when a friend's hand rests on my shoulder
and we keep driving until we get to a place with no memories
no currents, nothing
but new grass growing free from trees blocking out the sun

or the need of sprinklers.
I could make plants grow, I know I could be a gardener.

I know if we never get there
I could love seeing scenes with the top down

passing power lines and resistant rock, no other voices
in my head but one and it is laughing

and makes me want to laugh too.

Then there would be the porches we'd pass

people sitting at the end of day
the waitress who memorized our order

but then forgot the pancakes.
If we wanted, we could have pancakes

every evening, wherever we were
without feeling it a vice

or wishing we were more well-rounded.
Maple flavor lingering, maybe I'd fall asleep, maybe I
wouldn't.

Either way, we will go, we are already gone.
We will be gone forever

and still make it back before the dust rises
in daylight, another cloud with no rain.

George Thomas

Early November in The Poet's Ear

Poetry doesn't seem so very important when the first snow
Flies in autumn, and there's a heating bill to pay, and you're cold,
When the man up the road's dying of cancer and you love him.
Poetry's not important at all when the latest ex is full of
Bitterness bred of your neglect and your concentration on your art
To her exclusion. And what is poetry when you've lost the chance
To raise a lovely daughter, day by day, or carry the shame
Of sons abandoned long ago with another ex in a blind decision

You called freedom? Selfishness! Loss! So why continue scribbling
These pen tracks on blank white sheets like the dribbles
Of a spent cock? To put your name in some lit book nobody reads,
That most people shun as dull and pointless, as profitless? To make
A name among the nameless, to joust with giants only you make
giants in your fevered brain? Not one good, damned, logical,
          reasonable reason
To continue in this way, with this waste of life and sense, this
Frantic scribbling on this cave of paper wall with a charcoal stick!
          Why?
If I knew "why" then I'd know how to stop, know how to lay down
This instrument of loss and leaving and be still, let go the constant
Surrendering to the inevitable rush of words that come to fill
My head, my world with light and loveliness, and the beauty
Of the human voice, chanting spells aloud that transform winter
Into the mystery of death or red berries to drops of blood
In the white snow of remembrance, sound that changes
          pain and fear
Into strength and hope—all that noise which is the impulse
Of instinct, stumbling over the blind tongue into the world of sight!

Nathan Tompkins

On the Birth of an Empress

It was at the dawn of the world
when I dialed that landline telephone
my fingers strummed the buttons
as if they were the strings and frets
on a miniature lap dulcimer.

I wanted to see if you
had been freshly harvested
from the garden of your mother's womb.

Then, I was told I was the father
of a lovely baby girl. You.

I just wish I could have watched
you emerge, and welcome you
into this world, and clutched you,
as my lips whispered musical notes
into your outraged ears.

I was not there to see you born.
I did not stand beside your mother
as you came into the world as a Caesar
a shining empress, scoured in sterile light.

That doesn't mean that I don't imagine
my lips as they leave a moist trace
on your forehead, on your cheek,
on your lips, or on your tears.

Nor does it mean that I don't imagine
me tell you stories that force the giggles
to gush from your childish throat.

But it does mean that I imagine
myself as I clutch you to my chest,
and croak in a voice, guttural with tears:
I love you, Jacinta.

Proliferate These Doorways

Contagious enthusiasm clears paths
welcome arms open doors
aspire to be the torch
whose zest for wonder
paints this landscape teeming with possibilities.
Small insignificant flicker
holds infinite potential
the spirit to overcome
   transcend, soar
deeper truths
create a ripple
offer purification
such that I
such that We
   may become love.

Collective resolution
     rings souls
beyond coincidence
we are one
synchronized web
vibrating

Oh sacred spirit walker
feet washed
  of autopilot quicksand
breathe in breath of life
exquisite radiance
possible, probable even.

Is my center clear?
Am I out of the way?

Breathe in unconditional love
        be liquid flame
        expand vision
        ethereal
        astral
Physical manifestation of life
Proliferate
        these doorways.

Ric Vrana

Red Carmody

Mike Carmody belonged to the local chapter
of the Ancient Order of Hibernians
and was the regional spokesperson
for the Communist Labor Party.
Hilarious, hard drinking, sports fan, womanizer,
our friendship cemented by mutual admiration,
honed knife sharp by hours of polemical debate.
We chased women together in those years when
we had what they wanted and we knew it
though I got nervous when he started dating my sister.
The rest of our energies went into
fixing our junker cars or
writing articles for the party's newspaper.
"After the insurrection…" he'd begin many sentences.
He ran and won election as chief steward
in the tire plant as a Communist.
I was also chief steward in my shop

but was a straight AFL-CIO guy, preferring
to be the mortar between the blocks of ideologues.
Near the end of our days together in the NEOH
Mike could not forgive my reluctance to join the vanguard.
I left him almost a past-friend, though true brother.

During the Parrots Beak, second week in,
constant jungle firefight, by now, he knew,
well inside Cambodia,
they took him away from the mayhem,
sent him for R & R in Saigon
where he saw the papers screaming
of the thirteen shot at Kent State
where they knew he'd gone two years to school.

Two decades later, I was already in Seattle.
They moved Mike across country
 to the cancer center for desperate treatment.
Chemo doubled the size of his head, grotesque, hairless.
We cried when we reunited in that hospital room.
I was the last one of us he would ever see.
Agent Orange, Midwest, flag draped funeral.
His mother collapsed in my arms at the cemetery.

Julene Weaver

Sexual Revolution

In the mirror
it is the body she remembers
sexy as S and I and N
it is the fucking she remembers
full fledged

hot and bothered
screaming orgasms
S and I and N
that will never
come again

In the mirror
the body is constrained
now   scared
there is no more
free love   no more
S and I and N
free as the '60s
love revolution and
this is s and a and d
that reflects back
in her mirror

This body of love
that remembers
twisting hips
Amazon breasts
easy as S and I and N
into stray palms

The price paid
twofold in this new
world after the free
reign fledged orgasms
we remember   changed
world   condoms
AIDS   all a sign of
the future that came

Previously published in *Gertrude,* Summer 2009.

Ingrid Wendt

Some Words to Toss Your Direction

Call if the going gets rough, and always
the promise, *I will*. This
ritual has gone on for years. And still,
in these everyday waters that keep on rising over our heads,

one or the other keeps floundering, one or the other keeps
watch: twice

down, never a third or the cry
for rescue, this distance perhaps

the way of all balance, no need
for us both to go down. And still

the longing: one word of knowing
someone knows, tossed

out without a line to pull us back in,
without a thought to consequence.

One bright rescue helping us want to go on.

Previously published in *Evensong* (Truman State University Press, 2011).

John Sibley Williams

The Ripples

The low dry lake stretches decades around me.
Ringed vermilion stains where water once quivered.
I sling a stone across the surface and hope for ripples.
Under the same stars, the same weight. The hard earth
I cannot drink.

My great-grandmother is here,
frozen in the moment she first forgot my face.
There are weeds in the garden,
safely outside my window.

Someone who claims to be my father walks in my blood.
I pretend the echo is my own.
I pretend and in time believe.
My mother left before things hardened.

I read that there's sixteen inches of snow back home,
a town shriveled into letters
that no longer string together a name.

I still get its newspaper out here,
miles from any mailbox,
years from where I pretend to be,
and savor the moisture from its pages
like a stone left in my mouth.

A Reuniting

It is the knife edge of Halloween
and you will leave tomorrow.
The chill of this coast
invades your joints like mold,
fills your lungs with moss.

Your suitcase sways on the porch swing.
Even the house seems to list,
as if it were built of driftwood
instead of deadwood.
All night, I hold you
like dead leaves in my fists
until the moon gives up
on the last breath of yesterday
held in my lungs.

I help you down to the bay.
The day is unseasonably clear, almost tropical.
You perch on a log,
unclench in the heat.

The low tide has left a plain of wet sand and derelict trees.
I begin to build something in the hope of filling myself.
First a Kon-Tiki deck of driftwood.
Then, circular walls piled higher
that suddenly tumble down in a hollow rumble.
I build again, learn the tolerance of wood for staying in place –
finish an igloo of ribs and fingers
as the horizon harvests a pumpkin-sun.

I turn and you have crawled up a tangle of branches and
trunks – chasing the light upward from a darkened shore
your arms sunning out as if you want this brittle wood
to find buds and leaves.

Soon, my dome drifts out on the evening tide,
keeps itself intact as it twists.
The sun-burned Pacific promises
to set it on fire. I feel the breaking waves
at the bay's mouth in my legs, my ribs, my teeth
as they splinter this home
I cannot live in.

Previously published in *Word Riot*, May 2011.

Sally Wong

Crack Mom Blues

Her child needs her love. Does she not realize?
Through the legal proceedings, Mercy cried;
The toddler with downturned pout, squinty eyes.

Pink lipstick and business suit can't disguise
her gaunt face and cuttings concealed inside.
Her child needs her love. Does she not realize?

Unkempt home with sour milk and food with flies;
Cravings for crack caused her to set aside
the toddler with downturned pout, squinty eyes.

Lured by crispy green bills, she'd jeopardize
the child's safety by dealing drugs outside.

Her child needs her love. Does she not realize?

Investigators have exposed her lies,
and witnesses at court have testified (of)
the toddler with downturned pout, squinty eyes.

Choosing cocaine became her demise,
Custody lost; truth and justice preside.
Her child needs her love. Does she not realize?
The toddler with downturned pout, squinty eyes.

Carolyne Wright

Spokane Reservation School Teacher:
Welpinit, Washington

They used to have a dentist all day
Thursday. Now, you wait three months
or hitch to Spokane when the root's ache
breaks your stoicism down. Sharp operators
still cut Indians open at the B.I.A.
To live here, stay on automatic, keep
emergency systems on all night,
miss your lover only once a week.
When the bookmobile wheels in, hide there,
read how missionaries staked conversion
claims on tribes, worried at each others'
like tribe terriers over buffalo scraps.
Your school's an old God-trap of theirs,
earthed up now like a sod-sided council lodge.
Teenagers pass furtive peace pipes
through the fence at recess. If you weren't
the boss, brought from outside like a Jesus book,

you'd join them. Instead, you skirt the rules
like the obscene Salish scribbled
on latrine walls, follow the pretense
of coincidence, catch the braves red-handed.
Alright peace chiefs, back inside.
Finally Friday. You close the grade book
in the late light slanting over empty desks,
catch the last rush-hour rattletrap to town.
Your lover got the letter, thought it over,
lounges for you by the baggage counter.
All weekend you try to intersect
with something worth saying.
Sunday evening, it's like your blood's run thin,
your language dying, buffalo gone north.
Nowhere left but the reservation.
The white man leaves you at the depot;
one quick kiss and he's gone, remote
as a black robe, council fires smoking
on far bluffs, a leaf spinning into the night.
Now you know how they felt.

Previously published in *Stealing the Children* (Ahsahta Press, 1992).

Louise Wynn

Recovery

I
My mother needs to move
away, out of that house of
dark rooms and closed doors.

My grandmother wants us

safe, sound
her arms hold us
too tight.

I am little, lucky. I can play
inside and out
ignore the anger
avoid the gloom

Until I get
the sores and blisters.
"Don't turn on the light!"
"It will make your eyes weak."
"Sleep."
The dark room is good,
they agree (finally, on something).

II
How can I sleep through their simmering heat? It seeps under
the door with the light from the kitchen, streams in whenever
they open the door, looms outside like the pillar of salt my
mother would have turned into if she had looked back.

I stroke my bunny's soft pink ears. "We'll throw that away,"
says Grandma, but "No," my mother says, "we will not." And
she washes it tenderly in Borax and Castile soap and lets it
dry by the stove in the kitchen Grandma had not entered since
my sister got sick.

III
"See Sis's scars?" my mother warns me.
"That's from scratching. So don't scratch."

So I don't. I hold my
bunny and I don't scratch.
"She didn't get it as bad," said Grandma.
"No, she didn't," said Mother.

IV
And finally we moved, far away,
from the desert to the beach,
to big windows, light breeze.

My sister brought Grandma's picture. She put the pastel-
tinted photo in its gilt frame on her side of the wall. "What a
sad smile," said my sister. "She misses us." But I said, "She's
watching us. She's asking: 'How did you get away? Why
didn't you stay?'"

Now, my mother puts a cool washcloth on my face,
touches me with her soft hands, and
when the day gets too warm, lets me
spray cool water all around the patio
where light-spangled drops sparkle and dazzle my eyes
but certainly don't blind me.

GHOST TOWN POETRY OPEN MIC
Chronology of Featured Readers
2004-2013

Ice Cream Renaissance Featured Readers
2005

Thursday, May 12: David Madgalene

2006

Thursday, January 12: Brittany Baldwin
Thursday, March 9: Dennis Arlo Voorhees
Thursday, April 13: Marc Marcel
Thursday, July 13: Norma Mizer
Thursday, September 7: G.L. Morrison
Thursday, October 12: Flora Durham
Thursday, November 9: Ken Palmer (R.I.P.)
Thursday, December 7: Roy Seitz

Cover to Cover Featured Readers 2007

Thursday, January 11: Mary Szybist and Jerry Harp
Thursday, February 8: Tom Davis (R.I.P.) & Jim Templeton (piano)
Thursday, March 8: Danielle Champiet
Thursday, May 10: Ann Snyder and students from her Clark College Women's Studies class
Thursday, June 14: David Hill
Thursday, July 12: Poets from the River Poets anthology: Toni Partington, Sean McGill, Lee Powell, and Danielle Champiet
Thursday, August 9: Dan Raphael
Thursday, September 13: Paula Sinclair
Thursday, October 11: The Striped Water Poets Round Table of Auburn, Washington: Lana Hechtman Ayers, Maggie Kelly, and David Rizzi
Thursday, November 8: Sharon Wood Wortman

Thursday, December 13: Judith Montgomery

2008

Thursday, January 10: One year anniversary celebration
Thursday, February 14: Sage Cohen
Thursday, March 13: Paul Nelson
Thursday, April 10: Jack Kerouac School of Disembodied Poetics/Ginsberg reading with Kerouac School alumni John Chinworth, Christopher Luna, Marcus Mennes, and Shin Yu Pai
Thursday, May 8: Charles Potts
Thursday, June 12: Margareta Waterman
Thursday, July 10: Kyle David Congdon and Kori Sayer
Thursday, August 14: Paulann Petersen
Thursday, September 11: Jack Lorts
Thursday, October 9: Nancy Thompson
Thursday, November 13: David Hill
Thursday, December 11: Washington State Poet Laureate Sam Green

2009

Thursday, January 8: Second year anniversary celebration with book launch for Christopher Luna's chapbook, *GHOST TOWN, USA,* and postcard poets Lana Ayers, Diane Cammer, Eileen Elliott, Naomi Fast, and Maggie Kelly
Thursday, February 12: Catherine Warner
Thursday, March 12 – Friday, March 13: Lorraine Healey
Thursday, April 9: David Abel
Thursday, May 14: David Meltzer and Michael Rothenberg
Thursday, June 11: Jeff Lair
Thursday, July 9: Judith Arcana
Thursday, August 13: Jim Martin
Thursday, September 10: Eileen Elliott
Thursday, October 8: Sage Cohen
Thursday, October 29 – Friday, October 30: Neeli Cherkovski

Thursday, November 12: Melissa Beal
Thursday, December 10: Casey Bush

2010

Thursday, January 14: Third year anniversary celebration and book launch for Toni Partington's *Wind Wing*
Thursday, February 11: Laura Winter
Thursday, March 11: Barbara LaMorticella
Thursday, March 25, Saturday, March 27: Danika Dinsmore
Thursday, April 8: Walt Curtis and James Honzik
Thursday, May 13: Jack McCarthy (R.I.P.)
Thursday, June 10: Kristin Berger
Thursday, July 8: David Madgalene
Thursday, August 12: Sheryl Clough
Thursday, September 9: Ed Coletti
Thursday, October 14: Carlos Reyes
Thursday, November 11: Penelope Scambly Schott
Thursday, December 9: *VoiceCatcher 5* book launch with Jo Barney, Elizabeth Elfring, Lisa Maier, Kristin Roedell, and four of the artists whose work appears in the anthology: Anni Becker, April Bullard, Jane Poole, and Sara *

2011

Thursday, January 13: Fourth anniversary celebration with Richard Brautigan archivist and Washington State University Vancouver professor John Barber
Thursday, February 10-11: Turiya Autry
Thursday, March 10: Dennis McBride
Thursday, April 14: *Ghost Town Poetry* anthology book launch
Thursday, May 12: Carolyne Wright
Thursday, June 9: Michael Daley
Thursday, July 14: Tommy Gaffney
Thursday, August 11: Dan Nelson

Thursday, September 11: September 11 memorial reading with M and Christopher Luna

Tuesday, October 11: Uphook Press reading for the anthology *gape seed* with Judith Arcana, Christopher Luna, and Uphook Press editor Jane Ormerod

Thursday, October 13: John Amen

Thursday, November 10: Peter Ludwin

Thursday, December 8: *VoiceCatcher 6* reading with April Bullard, Deb Scott, Leah Stenson, Alice Hardesty, Dawn Thompson, and Meredith Stewart

2012

Thursday, January 12: Five year anniversary celebration with musical guests Jennifer Pratt-Walter, Bret Jorgensen, and Lincoln's Beard

Thursday, February 9: John Sibley Williams

Thursday, March 8: John Burgess

Thursday, April 12: Book launch for Jenney Pauer's *Serenity in the Brutal Garden*

Thursday, May 11: David Matthews

Thursday, June 14: Leah Stenson

Thursday, July 12: Patrick Bocarde and Melissa Sillitoe

Thursday, August 9: Anatoly Molotkov with guitarist Ragon Linde/ Premiere of Chris Martin's film about Christopher Luna, *Innovators of Vancouver* Season 2, Episode 1: http://www.innovatorsofvancouver.com/season2/christopher-luna/

Thursday, September 13: Julene Tripp Weaver

Thursday, October 11: Kristin Roedell and Traci Schatz (now Sidra Grace Quinn)

Thursday, November 8: Ric Vrana

Saturday, November 17: Great Weather for Media reading for the anthology *It's Animal But Merciful* with editor Jane Ormerod and contributors Richard Loranger, Christopher Luna, Dan Raphael, and Gina Williams

Thursday, December 13: Mary Slocum

Thursday, January 10: Six Year anniversary celebration with songwriter Matt Meighan and book launch for Eileen Elliott's *Miles of Pies*

Thursday, February 14: Amy Harper

Thursday, March 14: Brittney Corrigan

Thursday, April 11, 13: Kelly Keigwin and Sam Mackenzie

Thursday, May 9: Ingrid Wendt and Ralph Salisbury

Thursday, June 13: Raul Sanchez

Thursday, July 11: Dawn Thompson

Thursday, August 8: Stephanie Lenox and National Student Poet Miles Hewitt

Thursday, September 12: Doug Marx and Katharine Salzmann

Thursday, October 10: Rob Gourley

Thursday, November 14: Maggie Chula

Thursday, December 12: Christi Krug

Afterword

It is utterly impossible to summarize ten years of an open mic that has evolved beyond all expectations. Yet, as we present our second volume of poets from the series, it seems fitting to reflect upon what this monthly event means to us. It is where we come to practice and to hear how our poems sound. We hope to find like-minded people with whom to build community. The event gives us the opportunity to learn about other poetry readings, workshops, writers' groups, and submission calls. The community that gathers at Cover to Cover Books on the second Thursday of every month also serves as a second family for many. We've met many friends there, some whom have become friends for life. We've watched kids grow into professional performers. We've thrilled at new poets who have worked their craft into extraordinary books. We have laughed, cried, cringed, and loved so many fine moments. Perhaps most importantly, the reading remains all ages and uncensored. We are most proud of all of the community support that has kept the reading alive and well for ten years.

Christopher started the series because he was bored, and because he realized that creating what one would like to see in their neighborhood is more constructive than complaining about what it lacks. Toni began contributing great ideas behind the scenes in 2009 and was eventually persuaded to join him as co-host. The story of the success of this reading series runs parallel to the friendship and partnership that we have found in one another, and we see all of this as proof that poetry and love are never mutually exclusive.

We have been honored to call Cover to Cover Books home since 2007. Every month Mel Sanders keeps the doors open beyond the six o'clock closing time to host us. Over the years we developed a devoted group of regular attendees from Portland, despite the tendency among residents of that city across the river to stick close to home. Our audience typically swells to more than 40 people. Mel and Mark set up the chairs and prepare the setting, ready to make lattes and sell books. Cover to Cover feels like home to so many folks.

There are many businesses and individuals who have supported our efforts. It often feels as if the entire city of Vancouver is behind us. At the risk of leaving someone out, we'd like to express our heartfelt appreciation for the following: Mel and Mark Sanders; Leah Jackson, Greg Bee, and all the staff at Angst Gallery and Niche Wine and Art Bar; John Barber and Dene Grigar; Vancouver businesses Ice Cream Renaissance, Mint Tea, Moe's, Mon Ami, Everybody's Music, Urban Eccentric, North Bank Artists Gallery, Erik Runyan Jewelers, the Kiggins Theatre, I Like Comics, and The Catalyst; Kori Sayer and Marci McReynolds for opening their homes to us when a fire at the original bookstore location forced the series to go out on the road; Anni Becker, Chris Martin, Nathan Tompkins, Tiffany Burba-Schramm, Julian Nelson, Tina Tran, and all the other photographers and filmmakers who document Vancouver's vibrant arts scene; Clark County Historical Museum; Dr. Kandy Robertson and the staff at WSUV's Writing Center; Gallery 360 and the Mosaic Arts Alliance; Cara Cottingham at KOUG Radio; the *Vancouver Vector*; Sage Cohen; Paulann Petersen; Dan Raphael; Walt Curtis, Barbara LaMorticella, and Patrick Bocarde of KBOO's Talking Earth, for keeping poetry on the air and inviting the Ghost Town poets to join them on the air; Rich Lindsay of KBOO's Radio Lost and Found; Derek Fenner and Ryan Gallagher of Bootstrap productions; Crowd the Book founder Vishal Khanna in North Carolina; Great Weather for Media in New York; New Way Media and Big Bridge in California; and finally, the Arts of

Clark County and the Clark County Arts Commission for their tireless work to keep art alive in the hearts of every citizen.

So how do we sum up ten years of a shared experience? Perhaps to say thank you: for supporting us and one another; for showing up each month; for bringing a fresh voice each time; for your close attention; for loving and accepting (unconditionally) first time readers; for showing such deep respect to all of the featured readers; for buying books and coffee; for help putting away chairs; for spreading the word; for believing that poetry means something; and for your writing, which is perhaps the biggest gift of all.

Christopher Luna and Toni Partington
January 2014

About The Editors

Toni Partington

Toni Partington lives and works as a poet, editor, visual artist, and life/career coach in Vancouver, Washington. Her poetry has been published in *The Cascade Journal*, *VoiceCatcher* (editions 3 and 4), *OutwardLink.net*, *Perceptions*, and others. She is the author of two books of poetry, *Jesus Is A Gas* (2009), and *Wind Wing* (2010). She served on the editing team for *VoiceCatcher 4, 5, & 6*, an annual Pacific Northwest anthology of women writers. Toni is co-founder and editor, with Christopher Luna, of Printed Matter Vancouver, an editing and small press service.

Toni uses paint, pastels, found images and objects to create collaged visual art. She enjoys art collaborations, most notably when art and poetry find a common voice. Toni's art has been shown in Vancouver, Washington at Angst Gallery, North Bank Gallery, and Culture Control (2009 & 2010). As well, Toni has donated her art and jewelry pieces to several art auctions to benefit local nonprofit organizations.

Toni holds a BA degree in Social Work, an MA in Humanities with a major focus in Literature and Literary Editing, and postgraduate work in career development from the University of Oregon. Before embarking on other adventures, Toni spent over ten years teaching and advising women in transition returning to college.

Toni is involved in promoting poetry, writing, and art in Vancouver, WA with a lively pack of dogs, friends, and peers.

Blog: www.tonipoetryandart.wordpress.com
Email: tonipartington@gmail.com

Hit and Run

By Toni Partington

4 pm
September 15, 2009
St. Johns Road
Gordon Patterson
Age 50

Should not happen
one too many stricken
in hapless ways
by thundering herds
underneath hooves of
inflated rubber
two tons or more
steel and glass
don't mean to crush
their smaller cousins
        accidental swerve
        clipped by a side mirror
        maimed, flattened
        killed
in a narrow lane
off the sidewalk
in a neighborhood
        like ours
        like yours
plant a ghost bike
on the spot
wear a helmet
say "be careful"
to loved ones who
ride the risk

this is a bike town
that lacks respect for
two-wheeled friends
reflected by high beams
in moonlight

it wasn't Gordon's time
not on a Tuesday afternoon
neither late summer nor early fall
just a beautiful afternoon

when an 18 year old driver
lifted him to the sky
phantom wings carried him home
up the hill
a final time

Christopher Luna

Clark County Poet Laureate Christopher Luna is a poet, publisher, visual artist, teacher, and editor with an MFA in Writing and Poetics from the Jack Kerouac School of Disembodied Poetics at Naropa University in Boulder, Colorado. He is the co-founder, with Toni Partington, of Printed Matter Vancouver, an editing service and small press that serves Northwest writers. In 2011 Niche Wine and Art Bar and Angst Gallery proprietor Leah Jackson named him the poet laureate of her businesses. In 2012 Luna was the subject of *Innovators of Vancouver*, one in a series of films by Chris Martin showcasing pioneering Vancouver, WA artists, business owners, and community leaders.

Luna frequently collaborates with musicians. His spoken word recordings have been featured on Dr. Demento, Vin Scelsa's Idiot's Delight, and KBOO Portland's Radio Lost and Found, hosted by Rich Lindsay. His poetry has appeared in publications including *Twenty Four Hours Zine, The Understanding Between Foxes and Light, It's Animal But Merciful, Unshod Quills, Take Out, Night Bomb Review, Soundings Review, Chiron Review, Full of Crow, Cadillac Cicatrix, Gare du Nord, Exquisite Corpse, the @tached document*, and *Big Scream*. In April 2013 he created a poem per day based on Norman Mailer's 1980 Pulitzer-Prize winning novel *The Executioner's Song* for Pulitzer Remix, a National Poetry Month project sponsored by the *Found Poetry Review*.

Luna's articles and media criticism have appeared in the e-zine *Writing the Life Poetic* as well as *Rain Taxi Review of Books*, the *Columbian*, the *Oregonian, Willamette Week*, and the *Vancouver Vector*, among others. His books include *tributes and ruminations* (Dristil Press, 2000), *On the Beam* (with David Madgalene, 2005), *Sketches for a Paranoid Picture Book on Memory* (King of Mice Press, 2005), and *GHOST TOWN, USA* (This is Not an Albatross, 2008). *To Be Named and Other Works of Poetic License* (New Way Media, 2010), a poetic travelogue and art book created in collaboration with David Madgalene and Toni Partington was accompanied by an art show at Angst Gallery in Vancouver, WA displaying many of the one-of-a-kind covers for the book, each of which was made by altering an album cover. "More than we can bear," an epic investigative poem about the aftermath of September 11, was anthologized both online (*For Immediate Release*) and in print (*On the Way After 9/11*, 2002 and *Candles in the Dark, Flames for the Future*, 2003, ed. David James Randolph, New Way Media). Luna is also the author of *Literal Motion* (Bootstrap Press, 2001), which features three interviews with the filmmaker Stan Brakhage. In May 2011 Big Bridge published *The Flame Is Ours: The Letters of Stan Brakhage and Michael McClure 1961-1978*, an important piece of Twentieth-Century literary and cinema history that Luna compiled and edited at Brakhage's request.

Christopher Luna recently launched Crowd the Book, a crowdsourcing service for small press authors and publishers and the readers who love them, with his fellow Kerouac School alum Vishal Khanna.

Blog: http://christopherluna-poetry.blogspot.com
Email: christopherjluna@gmail.com

Loving Poetry Is Like Being A Fan of Horror Movies
By Christopher Luna

> so enamoured with the genre
> that you are willing to sit through movies that are
> completely moronic
> and not-at-all scary
> in the hopes of catching
> that one unique concept
> or cool character
> or original way of dispatching with someone
> (the basketball which completely obliterates a person's head
> in that piece of shit *Deadly Friend*
> or the fully grown adult male who claws
> his way out of the woman who has been raped
> by an alien in *Xtro*)
> you stick with it to the end
> because you love it

fully realizing that they can't all be
The Exorcist, *The Omen*, or
Night of the Living Dead
can't all be Cronenberg, Argento,
Lewton, Whale, or Carpenter,
dig?

About Printed Matter Vancouver

Printed Matter Vancouver is a small publishing press for poets and writers interested in taking their work to the next level. The next level for most writers is to see their work in print; in other words, to get published. In 2010 we took our love of writing, editing, and mentoring writers to our natural next step: to create a service that assists the writer in preparing their work for public consumption. It was then that we created Printed Matter Vancouver.

Printed Matter Vancouver provides writing and editing services for poets and writers interested in submitting their work for publishing consideration to a small press, journal, anthology, contest, or for self-publishing. We work one-on-one with writers to assist with edits, format, content, arrangement, and submission strategies.

We work on small and large projects — from broadsides and chapbooks to collections and anthologies. We are formally trained and published writers/editors/poets who believe in writing as a lifestyle. We are committed to showcasing the best writing the Pacific Northwest has to offer. Let us help you launch yourself and make your writing goals a reality. Our fees are below scale because as fellow poet Ed Coletti says, "there's no money in poetry." We agree and would like to add; even though poets aren't getting rich these days, they're writing with heart and passion and yes, changing the world as they go.

Christopher Luna and Toni Partington
Editors, Printed Matter Vancouver
www.printedmattervancouver.com
printedmattervancouver@gmail.com

Christopher Luna & Toni Partington
Editors/Publishers
Printed Matter Vancouver

Photo By Julian Nelson, 2013